ALL ABOUT ME AND THE THINGS I CAN DO, NOW THAT

I AM FOUR!

Words by Peter Jarrette and Dorothy Rose
Pictures by Anthony Rao

Little Simon
Published by Simon & Schuster, New York

Text copyright © 1982 by Little Simon,
a Simon & Schuster Division of Gulf & Western Corporation.
Simon & Schuster Building, 1230 Avenue of the Americas, New York, New York 10020.
Illustrations copyright © 1982 by Anthony Rao.
Printed in U.S.A.   0-671-44468-9

Today is my birthday—I'll shout and I'll roar,

I'm big as a lion—hooray, I am four!

I love to get messy with colors so bright,
The red and the yellow, the blue and the white.

I know all my letters from A straight through Z,
And reading short words is so easy for me.

The books that I have are all up on the shelf,
They look very big, but I read them myself.

My favorite game is called hide-and-go-seek,
I cover my eyes and I try not to peek.

I search for my friends as they hide all about,
Or stand by the goal and try tagging them out.

We're searching for fish,
Salamanders, and frogs,
For lizards, and bugs,
And small pollywogs.

We went on a hike and we found something new,

A barn filled with hay
And some cows that said "moo."

The garden's a great place
To play as I please,
I dig up some worms
And get mud on my knees.

I'm planting a seed
That will be a big squash,

And after I'm done,
I'll help Mom with the wash.

I go to the Doctor
And don't cry or yell,
He'll give me a lolly
And help keep me well.

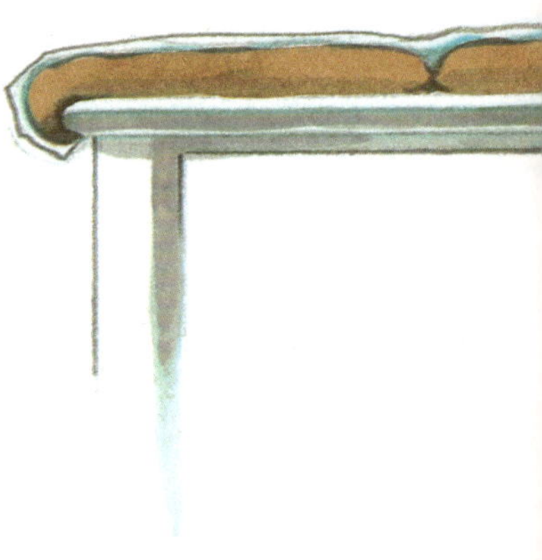

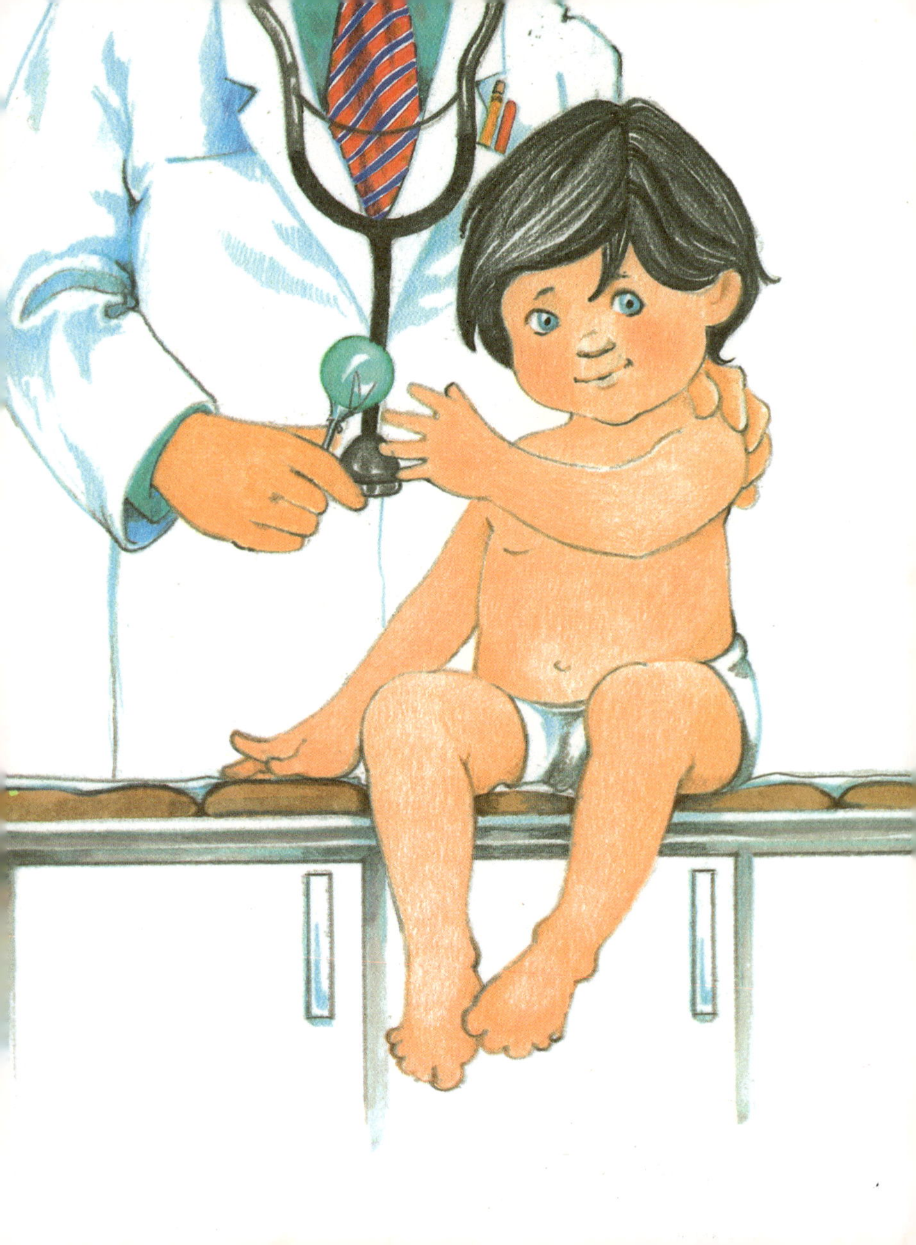